Karli's Kritters

Story and Photography by

JAN CAMMARATA

AuthorHouse™
1663 Liberty Drive
Bloomington, IN 47403
www.authorhouse.com
Phone: 833-262-8899

Because of the dynamic nature of the Internet, any web addresses or links contained in this book may have changed
since publication and may no longer be valid. The views expressed in this work are solely those of the author and do not
necessarily reflect the views of the publisher, and the publisher hereby disclaims any responsibility for them.

This book is printed on acid-free paper.

ISBN: 978-1-4389-6726-4 (sc)

Print information available on the last page.

Published by AuthorHouse 09/28/2022

authorHOUSE®

For My BC Boy
From the streets of Washington DC
to my heart, I will always miss you.

When you disappeared I looked everywhere
except the building in which you were trapped.
Cats don't leave their food source. Never stop
looking for your missing cat. He is nearby but
just can't get back to you.

Millions of feral and friendly street cats are
hiding in our cities. You can help.
Spay and neuter your pets and help
feral homeless cats by learning about
TNR at www.alleycatallies.org

Remember, when you buy a dog or cat
you destroy the chance of life of one in a
shelter. Five days isn't very long. Be
responsible. Please check www.petfinder.com.

I'm Karli, and I'm so lucky!
I have a lot of wonderful pets because
my mom is an animal rescuer.

My dog Simon is my best friend. Mom got him from a man who didn't want to take care of him anymore.

Simon lets me put my head on him like a pillow when I read or watch TV.

When I want to run, we chase each other around the yard.

Someone else gave up Sammy, and my mom brought her home from the shelter for unwanted dogs.

She and Simon love each other very much.

She loves me too, because after
she growls at me for being so wild,
she kisses me on the face.

My cat Gigi is deaf.
She is black and white like a penguin.

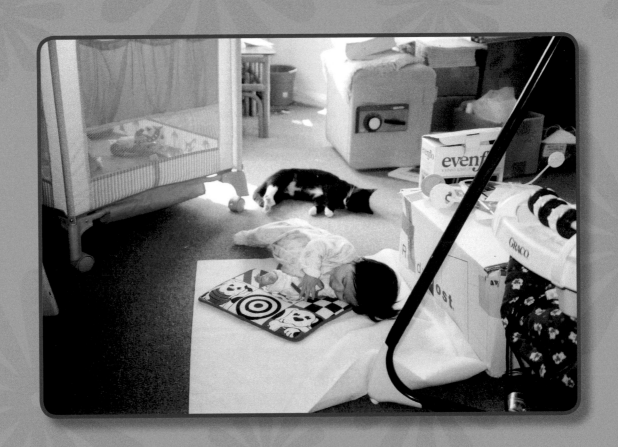

She likes me too, but mom says it's because
she can't hear me when I'm playing a little loud.

Howard is a black cat with a tooth sticking out.

We play in my Dora the Explorer tent until he thinks my toes are a toy . . . ouch!

My cat Buzzy and his cross-eyed sister Zoie, were rescued from the streets of Washington DC.

They both think Simon the dog is their mother.

Buzzy sometimes plays too hard with a bird or a mouse, so Mom tries to save them, too!

There are many people who don't take good care of their pets, so people like my mom and me have to rescue them and help find them a forever home.

Even Oprah was on television asking people to try to adopt dogs and cats from shelters so they don't have to live in a cage forever. I like her.

I'm adopted too. My mom rescued me from Guatemala, but she says I was the one who really rescued her.

It feels good to help!

THE END

In memory of Luke

One of the biggest loves in my mom and dad's life
(after my brother and me).